WICCA CANDLE MAGIC

Basic Candle Magic for Newbies includes a few easy-to-follow Candle Spells

(2022 Guide For Beginners)

Wendy Oliver

SECTION 1

FIRE'S MAGNIFICENCE

OUR RELATIONSHIP WITH FIRE

Have you ever been labelled a pyro in school or teased for your love of fire? The fact is that you are not the only person who likes fire. Because fire is one of the elements, it plays an important role in the Wiccan tradition. We are so inextricably linked to fire because it is a part of nature. We are tied to the ground, but we may be even more attached to fire because it is such an important part of our lives and spells.

Fire dances across the landscape as though nothing can get in its way. It is both deadly and beautiful, and if that doesn't put you in a state of scared awe, I don't know what would. Because fire is one of nature's most enthralling miracles, our capacity to connect with it is astonishing. Why do humans have such a strong bond with fire? Perhaps because, like us, it is completely misunderstood or dismissed as irrelevant. Or maybe it's because it's such an important element of so many spells. We spend so much time with it during spells that we've formed an attachment to it. There are several hypotheses as to why we have a connection with the fire, and none of them is right. The ultimate fact is that it is an important component of many Wiccan ceremonies, which is why candles are utilised.

CANDLES ARE USED IN WICCAN RITUALS.

Candles are frequently used in various spells, but they are especially important in ritual magic.

Proper ceremonial magic will require you to begin your circle with a candle representing each element, as well as a white candle for cleansing.

Candles are among the items required by a Wiccan to accomplish the bulk of spells. They are constantly there and never going to waste. Even while they are not required, some Wiccans like to start their circles with candles every time rather than simply invoking the elements, which is fine. If you have the time, it's not a bad idea to put up the candles every time. If you've gotten this far in the Wicca series and still don't understand the value of candles, this book will alter your mind. As this is the fourth book in the series, you've already read about several spells that use candles, but there are additional rituals that rely only on candles. Most people think of herbs when they think of Wicca spells and magic, but candles may be just as potent if used appropriately.

Wiccans frequently utilise candles to bring them wealth or protection, or for any number of other reasons that they require a ritual to be cast. Candles are sometimes used to ignite smudge sticks since they have the most stable flames.

Candles provide natural light at your fingers and may be utilised to discover items. You may even do a protection spell using the same candle that you're using for lighting. Candles may also be used to heat things, such as herbs, when they need to be warmed up so that they are primed and ready to use. When it comes to candles, there aren't many restrictions.

MAGIC OF THE FIRE

Fire magic is magic that is created by employing fire itself, rather than the colour of a candle. This spell invokes the element fire. A warming spell is an example of a fire spell when we are outside in the cold. Fire magic is extraordinary because it allows you to feel the warmth of fire even when you are not near an open flame.

To employ fire magic, you must be willing to work with an element that does not have a circle. This may quickly spiral out of control and requires a lot of experience. However, if you are willing to put in the effort, you will discover that you are capable of doing some remarkable things. Many Wiccans believe that you cannot truly harness the power of the elements, and this is true to some extent based on my observations. For example, you cannot start a fire without a spark, but once you have a little ember, you may summon fire to emblazon it and keep it blazing for a long time.

You may even summon fire to assist you in lighting that annoying pilot light on your heater. Witches have also invoked fire to shield you from harm. It's a bit frightening how many spells exist for channeling the sheer force of fire. With how unpredictable fire can be, if everyone tried them all at once, things may get out of hand.

THE IMPORTANCE OF COLOR

Colour is very essential in candle magic. If you use the wrong colour candle and try to cast magic, you may have an entirely different outcome. You may be attempting to obtain more money, but if you light a blue candle, you might wake up with longer hair—you never know. Hues are significant; in Wiccan tradition, candles come in just five different colours. The colours black and grey are reserved for darker magic, and neither will be explored in this book. You will also employ colour subsets such as pink and orange. While Green and Purple are also considered secondary or subgroup hues, each of them is a primary in Wicca due to their elemental symbolism.

Blue candles can improve knowledge. You utilise them when you want to learn more about the world and open your mind to accepting the knowledge that you would otherwise reject. When coupled with a green candle, blue candles can offer you pleasure and wealth. This candle may also be used for a variety of different purposes, such as assisting you in dealing with difficult situations.

GREEN

Green candles are referred to as money candles. It provides you with money and success. If you want to create more money, there are a million spells out there, and I'm sure 90% of them involve you utilising a green candle in some way. It also aids in healing. It can aid in the healing of your diseases, just as it may aid in the repair of your shattered finances. It has the power to bring more love into your life while also banishing immorality. Green is a sign of new beginnings and hope.

YELLOW

Yellow candles are commonly referred to as "pick me up" candles. What comes to mind when you think about the colour yellow? You imagine sunlight, daffodils, daisies, and a plethora of other bright and cheerful things, don't you?

Yellow is excellent for preventing depression or pulling a depressed individual out of a near-catatonic condition. Yellow candles may also bring joy and vitality into a place. Yellow is excellent for strengthening the mind, spreading compassion, and attracting new connections.

RED

This is the hue of fervor. Of fortitude. Of bravery. This is the colour you see when you are so angry that you want to shout, and it is also the colour you feel when you are so in love with someone that your heart feels like it is going to burst. Red instils vitality in a space. It also provides motivation. Because of the energy, courage, and power that red candles impart, they are utilised in many motivational spells.

PINK

This candle is nearly only used for love charms. Pink is associated with withdrawing love. Not only from others but also from yourself. It is also for personal success. It may help you achieve success in a variety of undertakings, whether they are business or romantic.

ORANGE

It is a blend of yellow and red that represents passion and pleasure. It seems to reason that this hue would be ideal for restoring damaged relationships and friendships. It also works well when combined with a yellow candle to bring joy into the atmosphere.

PURPLE

This is the hue of foresight. The hue of prophecy. The hue of magic in its purest form. This hue depicts Spirit, the guiding light and the source of our magic. This hue may heal emotional suffering that has accumulated over time and is a nice relaxing colour. It can be used for meditation. It will provide you with inner serenity, allowing you to concentrate. Not to add that it is a gorgeous colour in general because of the numerous distinct tints that it comes in, none of which are even substantially identical.

WHITE

White candles are used for protection, cleansing, and healing. When performing a ceremony that involves bloodletting, a white candle should be lit. You are delivering your DNA to whatever takes up your blood as an offering, and your blood might be presented to an evil entity if you do not use a white candle or cleansing. You can protect yourself by lighting a white candle. It forms a barrier to keep unwelcome spirits at bay.

Colour is very important in magic. Each hue has its attribute, and each attribute is distinct. Choose the appropriate hue to get the desired effect. Choose a colour to focus your attention on since it is not just about the colour, but also about the energy associated with it and how strongly your energy is related to the energy of the candle. Stay focused on what you want the spell to accomplish, and if you attempt to send your energy out to every candle, you will run into issues since your energy will not be as powerful as it would be if you only focused on one candle. The only exception is if you need to burn the five elements plus the white candle for a ritual, or if you need to combine two candles for a specific spell to make it more potent. Follow the spell if your magic just requires one candle colour. Always double-check that you have the correct colour.

CANDLE MAGIC PREPARATION

CANDLES FOR SPELL CASTING

There are several sorts of candles that may be burned. However, only a few varieties are well-suited to the witch community. If you don't need to designate it with symbols or charge it, feel free to use any type. (That is, a lower-level spell) However, after you reach a higher level of candle magic, you will require specific types of candles.

There are large and little tea light candles, as well as small and medium glass-encased candles, chub candles, and taper candles. Because your possibilities are so broad, they might become complicated after a time, thus this section will serve as a guide to assist you in determining which candles you require to make your spells easier and more successful.

LARGE CHUB CANDLES

Big chub candles are the type that you'd place in a lovely glass dish. They're a little plump and either flat on top or tapered. It is entirely dependent on who creates them. These are ideal when you need the flame to burn a long time and when you need to carve a sign into it since it has a large enough surface area to carve a symbol clearly without worrying about it being too obscure to be effective.

CANDLES FOR SMALL CHUBS

These are useful for when you need a candle to burn rapidly but also need to carve a symbol into it. Because their burn period is much shorter than that of a huge chub, this is the method to go if you need to burn a candle all the way down in one shot and don't have a lot of time.

LARGE TAPER

If you've ever seen a menorah, you'll recognize a taper candle. These candles are long and slim, and they grow thinner as they rise. If you don't need to carve a symbol, they are ideal. They burn quickly and are exceedingly attractive, much more so than regular candles due to their sleek appearance. If you have the time to let them burn down or if you can use them for more than one ritual, these are the ones you use for spells that don't require a sign carving.

TAPERING TO A POINT

These are a little tougher to come by if it isn't near to the Christmas season, so stock up. These little, slim candles are ideal for witch bottles since you must allow the flame to burn out, which necessitates the use of a small candle. Bottle corks are an option, but they're typically tiny, and a chub wouldn't work for a witch bottle. Because you don't need a sign on your candle, a little taper is ideal.

CANDLES FOR TEA LIGHTS

These candles are useful for summoning the elements, especially if they are coloured. They burn for a short period, yet long enough for you to do a spell, and there are large tea lights if the ritual takes hours. In most locations, stock up on colourful ones in the spring because that is when they appear to be out regularly.

GLASS-ENCASED CANDLES

These are not appropriate for use in a Wiccan ritual. They are merely for adornment, and the smells that are frequently put in them are not natural and can disrupt the balance of your spell. You want to use only natural candles in your spells to keep the energy balanced.

SELECTING A CANDLE

Using the preceding part as a guide, it should be easy to decide what candle you require in terms of form and colour. However, there are many more factors to consider while selecting a candle. Consider where you will do the rite. What kinds of candle holders do you have on hand? How simple is it to remove wax? Have the correct candle so you may concentrate your efforts on the candle and not on messes, fire, or any other threat that may develop. If you are in a dry location, keep a pail of water nearby to put out a fire if a candle falls over and sets something on fire. You want to have everything ready in case of necessity so that when you light the candle and begin the spell, you can relax.

Pay close attention to how a candle is made. If it is not made with natural materials, you should avoid using it because Wicca is all about being as natural as possible. You want candles made of soy wax rather than paraffin wax. In a pinch, paraffin wax can be used, however, it can cause some imbalance difficulties with the spell.

You should also go out and get the candles rather than ordering them online since you want to select candles that work with your energy. Inanimate items may appear strange to mesh with, but trust me, much like your book of shadows, you want to be compatible with the candles that you purchase. Choose a brand and stay with it because they are all made in the same way.

BEING REALISTIC

Use your candles for practical purposes. You cannot expect to cast a spell with the power of a level 10 expert simply by purchasing a candle. You must put forth the effort.

Many individuals abandon magic because they do not believe it works for them. They're looking for riches with money magic, so they don't notice the random change that's just sitting about.

Instead, they hope to locate a duffel bag full of cash. This is an example of being unpractical. If you're casting riches magic, take attention to the pennies you find and the strange places they keep appearing. Consider where you obtained the dime. With your magic, be patient and realistic. Otherwise, you will eventually abandon candle magic.

YOUR CANDLES ARE BEING CONSECRATED

Prepare and cleanse your candles before using them. While certain spells may require less in-depth candle consecration than others, it is vital to understand the core of the spell before attempting it.

CLEARING

You must extinguish all of your candles. You should clean your candles before putting them away.

Wash them with warm water and cast a cleaning charm on them, such as

The ability of water to wash this candle creates a blank slate.

Simple chant with no rhyme, yet it cleanses the candle of any residue from the outer world.

Clearing allows your candles to become pure again, regardless of any impurities they have come into contact with during production and handling, or even just resting on shop shelves. You want candles that are transparent and have no associations with anything, almost like a blank slate. This helps you to get the most energy out of your candle, which is useful in your aspirations as a novice witch.

CHARGING

Not all spells need the use of a charged candle, but it is a good idea to practice with one on hand. If you have a spell, such as a witch bottle, you don't need a charged candle since the magic is done by fire mixed with colour, coupled with what's within the bottle. You must charge your candle for spells that rely only on candle magic. To do so, you must first ensure that it is obvious.

Then you have to wait for a new moon. The new moon represents a new beginning, which is what you want for your candles. Unlike with crystals, where you want a full moon to charge your candle, you want a new moon to charge your candle like a clean slate so that it is ready for any spell you need.

Say a spell over your candles just before placing them in a window or outside to allow them to be charged. You may utilize one like the Vessel of fire take in the darkness and let it charge you and make you dazzling. It doesn't have to be complicated; it only needs to light the candle for the next moon cycle. Certain spells may require you to charge your candle during a different moon phase, but the procedure remains the same.

Allow it to charge and place it in front of the moon.

ANOINTING

A majority of spells need you to anoint your candle with oil-related to the spell. These might be oils like good luck or protective oils.

When you anoint the candle, make sure to rub the oil into it rather than simply pour it on it. Rub the oil in the desired direction of the spell. If you want the magic to come to you, massage the oil into the candle from the farthest side away from you and work your way in. If you want the enchantment to spread, begin at the candle side nearest to you and work your way out.

Anointing is used frequently, but not in all spells. Be prepared to use it frequently.

SYMBOLS FOR CARVING

Some spells, usually those of a higher degree, need you to carve symbols into your candles. These symbols are used to steady the flow of energy to prevent a calamity from occurring or to prevent the wrong creature from answering the call of your spell. Much higher-level spells have a greater broadcasting range than a direct line to the Goddess herself, and there is a lot of evil out there that can answer the call. Symbols assist you in maintaining a direct relationship to the Goddess rather than putting out a free-range signal that invites evil. If you must carve a sign into your candle, you should light a white candle just in case. Better to be cautious than sorry.

If you want to carve a symbol into your candle, use a clean, sharp knife blade (but anything sharp will do). You want whatever you're using to be clean, such as an X-ACTO knife blade, which will offer you precise cuts without requiring you to try again. Also, before you ruin a candle, practice carving out the design on a scrap piece of wax. Meltdown the stubs of old candles and pour them into a square mound to produce these scrap blocks. Once you've mastered carving the design into wax, you can go on to the candle, saving you money on candles.

TIMING

When consecrating your candles, keep in mind that some rituals may only be performed at specific times of the year. Make certain that you do not overlook the time, since this might convert a brilliant spell into a fizzle. In the magical realm, time in hours is immaterial; time in moon cycles is critical, and ignoring the moon cycle might lead to serious difficulties.

SPELLS & CANDLE MAGIC

GETTING GOING

To begin, make sure you have an assortment of candles on hand, as some spells will not work without them. Make sure you have all of the colours you'll need in all of the sizes and shapes you'll need. A Wiccan's storeroom usually appears like it was thrown up in by a candle business. If you're short on cash, store up a little at a time until you're ready to cast your spell.

If it proves to be more cost-effective, you may even produce your candles. If you want to transform a room in your house into a candle-making workshop, by all means, avoid commercial enterprises and go as near to nature as possible. In the Wiccan community, it is encouraged. Make sure you have all you need to dedicate your candles. When you reach that point, you'll need materials like oils and tools to carve symbols. You want to be able to just grab and go anytime you need a spell, rather than running about attempting to find the items you require.

Once you've prepared for a candle apocalypse, it's time to try some simple candle magic spells.

SPELLS OF LOVE

Love spells are tough because many people believe they may make someone fall in love with them even if they do not want to. That is not possible. Be cautious of your motives when casting love magic. You can only make someone fall madly in love with you, and when the enchantment wears off, it may go one of two ways. They either come to their senses or regard you as an outcast for breaching fundamental morality norms, or they become dangerously infatuated with you, to the point where they would kill you if it meant they could keep you with them forever. There's a reason why whenever you visit a genie, he says he can't make someone fall in love with you.

Wiccan love spells to assist you in finding your genuine love as well as love inside yourself, for yourself. These love charms are within the bounds of fundamental morality and are recommended. There is a fine line between morality and immorality, and love spells usually cross it.

LOVE ATTRACTION SPELL IN THE MOONLIGHT

This spell is intended to assist you in attracting love in your direction. While it may not immediately bring you your true love, it will bring you people worth loving. You wish to utilise this charm to attract love into your life. Attempting to limit the spell might cause it to fail in unexpected ways.

What you'll require

❖ A full moon,

❖ a pink candle,

- ❖ love,

- ❖ oil

- ❖ matches

Make a circle and stand in the center. Light the candle with the matches after anointing it with the love attraction oil. Make sure your circle is in the light of the moon, and then recite this chant.

Look down from above, Goddess of Grace, Fertility, and Love, and shower me with thunderous happiness and love; nothing less is acceptable. Take my life and resurrect me.

After you've recited this spell, let the candle burn out in the moonlight while you sit meditating. While you meditate, mentally send forth your prayer for love. When the candle burns out, shut your circle, gather your objects, and properly dispose of what you used up.

FINDING THE RIGHT PARTNER

This spell will assist you in finding your ideal love. You should apply this charm with caution and without thinking of anyone in particular. You must enter a spell with a clean slate. Otherwise, you risk casting bad love magic.

What you'll require

- ❖ pink wax candle
- ❖ a candle in yellow
- ❖ Matches white
- ❖ candles

Begin by arranging your pink, yellow, and white candles in a triangle. Cast your circle when you've done it. Each candle should be lit with a new match each time. After you've ignited them, recite this magic.

I beseech you, o great ones, to hear my scream and locate me the one who will complete my life, in whom I place my confidence.

Bring my one true love into my house just via you.

After then, you may blow out the candles and watch the smoke vanish. When all of the smoke has dissipated, you may shut your circle and tidy up.

ENHANCE YOUR RELATIONSHIP

If you are in a relationship and are like most couples, things seem to become a little dull after the first year, and while you may love your significant other, you want some more excitement in your life. You are not alone in your feelings. Everyone wants to spice things up a little, but they often don't know how or are too afraid to do so. This spell will assist in reviving items in the bedroom. This enchantment requires the use of both plants and candles, so get your herbs ready as well.

What you'll require

- ❖ cinnamon
- ❖ carnation
- ❖ hibiscus
- ❖ pink wax candle
- ❖ a single red candle

❖ fireproof mortar

❖ pestle bowl

To begin this spell, pound your herbs in a mortar and pestle and place them in a fireproof bowl. Cast your circle once you have those ready. Use the same match to light your red and pink candles. After you've lighted your candles, recite this magic.

Love is weary and old; take my love and make it bold.

Take your crimson candle and ignite the herbs as you speak bravely. Allow roughly half of them to burn before blowing them out. Then conclude the spell with this.

Bring back the butterflies, wipe away the tears, and give me fun for the rest of our lives.

Take the pink candle and ignite the remaining herbs as you say for years. Allow the herbs to burn out before blowing out your candles and sealing your circle.

SPELLS FOR MONEY

Money spells are not what you think they are. You will not become a millionaire by employing magic, and if you want to do so, you better put this book down now before you are disappointed. If you know someone who says that magically made them wealthy, it is likely that they employed black magic and are now suffering the price.

Use these charms for realistic purposes, not for out-of-this-world fantasies, as they will never live up to your expectations. The spells in this book are only intended to work for those who apply them exactly as written. That is, to assist you in achieving success and earning more money.

SPELL FOR QUICK POCKET CHANGE

This magic will assist you in locating additional money in your life, such as pennies, nickels, dimes, and even quarters. This spell will not bring you a hundred dollar note, and if you discover one, you should probably seek for the person who dropped it. This spell is not intended to bring you wealth.

What you'll require

- ❖ a light green candle

- ❖ A coin that attracts money

- ❖ oil

Cast a circle to begin this spell. Anoint your candle with money attraction oil and direct it toward you. Light the candle and drip a few droplets onto the coin, taking caution not to burn yourself (quarters appear to work best for this because they have a larger surface area). To fix the candle to the coin, use the wax on the coin. Say this spell when it burns down.

- ➢ Green candle, money bringer

I don't need much, just what you can spare me, a quarter here, a dime there, even some pennies if you have some to spare, I beg of you.

> ➤ I'd want to thank you in advance.

When the candle has burned out, you may seal your circle and remove the candle leftovers from your coin. Store as much melted wax on it as possible, and then place the coin where you keep your change. Keep an eye out for the transition.

GETTING RID OF MONEY OBSTACLES

This spell assists you in removing any impediments in your path, such as debt. After casting this spell, you may discover that some of your debt has been forgiven, or that something happened and a collection agency lost your file, so you no longer owe. If you are unemployed, you may discover that the job you have been looking for is now hiring. There are numerous ways for this spell to function, so if it doesn't work the way you want it to, don't be disheartened; it might be working on something much better for you.

What you'll require

- ❖ a light green candle
- ❖ 3 pieces of the fireproof paper bowl

Cast a circle to begin this spell. Invite the elements to join you in this spell, rather than simply asking them to protect you while you do it. Fold the three pieces of paper into three cubes and set them in the fireproof bowl. These cubes symbolize the "blocks" of money in your path. Light a green candle and recite this spell.

I beseech thee, the fire of power, to remove these terrible impediments from my path.

After you've uttered the spell, light the green candle and set fire to the blocks. After they have burnt out, blow out your green candle and shut your circle, thanking the element for participating in the 148.

SPELLS OF HEALING

Healing spells are harder to cast, hence the ones covered in this book will be for simple alleviation of maladies such as sprains, colds, or depression. These diseases are easily alleviated with simple charms that do not need specialist knowledge.

Healing spells frequently necessitate the use of a green candle as well.

SIMPLE CURE SPELL

This spell is just for you to use. It can help you recover from a sprain or a regular cold. This spell is fairly effective, and you will feel relief in a short time.

What you'll require

- ❖ a light green candle
- ❖ Nutmeg chamomile
- ❖ Matches in lavender.
- ❖ a teabag
- ❖ cup of boiling water

Unless your damage is severe, you do not need to cast a circle for this spell. You can complete these steps without a circle for minor problems.

Light a green candle and recite this spell.

> A green candle makes me feel better.

> Tea with numerous leaves makes me well, thus, I say, let it be.

After you've lighted the candle and spoken the spell, you can brew and drink your tea using the plants specified above.

GETTING RID OF DEPRESSION

This spell aids in the removal of depression. While it does not cure depression, and if you are suffering from it, you should get professional assistance, it does help with day-to-day problems, such as getting out of bed in the 149th minute.

What you'll require

- ❖ a candle in yellow
- ❖ long enough to make a bracelet out of yellow ribbon

Make a circle with your hands and light the yellow candle. Other than casting your circle, this spell does not require you to speak. Make the ribbon into the size of a bracelet that will easily glide on and off your wrist but will not fall off without effort at any point. Once you've found the right fit, sew the ends of the bracelet together using a lighter. Blow out the candle and hold the bracelet in the smoke until it fades. Put the bracelet back on and think about something

pleasant.

USING SPELLS TO IMPROVE YOUR LIFE

USING SPELLS TO IMPROVE YOUR LIFE

The goal of becoming a witch is to improve your life. This is something you can accomplish using magic. You may find yourself completely immersed in a new and more exciting way of living. It takes a lot of practice to improve your life using magic.

Most people do not naturally possess the ability to perform magic. To do anything, you must first get out of your brain. Life improvement is a huge aspect of Wiccan culture, and that's what attracts a lot of people to it. However, despite the fact that many people are drawn to this religion, many individuals abandon it as well, and this is because they are unwilling to put in the work when it comes to improving their life. They believe that all they have to do is speak a few words and the magic will happen. This is due, in part, to how magic is portrayed in the media. Consider the popular television show Charmed. It depicts three witches fighting evil with only a few easy spells, which is not true. The same may be said for the majority of available material. Wiccans are represented as folks who gather in the woods, recite a few spells, wave a few herb sticks, and then—bam—magic. It is more difficult than these depictions suggest.

Spells require skill and repetition to perfect the outcomes. There are also multiple distinct aspects to spells that you must learn before moving on to the next level and practicing those spells for hours on end before you receive any results. To become a strong witch, you must devote a significant amount of time and effort to your craft. The cost of being lazy will keep you at the same level for a long time.

Life improvement will not make your life more enjoyable. This is another reason why people abandon Wicca. They anticipate to be able to make their crush fall in love with them and utilise magic to become wealthy, but this does not occur—at least not straight away. Those things need a great deal of effort and attention. People have also joined and then abandoned the bandwagon by becoming dark witches. They figured out how to make themselves wealthy while also forcing someone to fall in love with them. That magic, however, comes at a cost, and it is not cheap. To get what they desire, some folks will literally sell their souls to a monster. You should avoid these witches at all costs. If a person died as a result of a black witch, their spirit would be tortured for all eternity. You will not be reborn; instead, you will be banished to purgatory.

Purgatory is the eternal destination for the spirits of those who have done evil and committed black magic. It's not where you want to be. Every day until the end of time, your spirit will be ripped apart, and even though your body will be dead, you will still be alive to experience it because you are your spirit. Let those who embrace Wicca and join the black witches' parish do so of their own volition.

Anyway, how do you use magic to improve your life? You make a connection with the earth. You make connections with other individuals. You surround yourself with things that will enrich and delight you. With magic, these things are conceivable. It may appear like magic cannot achieve anything that you cannot do yourself, and this may be true in some cases. However, being a Wiccan makes it much simpler to achieve these tasks with magic rather than without magic.

Creating New Friends - Friendship is difficult to come by, and even if you have a large number of friends, they may not be the ideal kind of friends to have. We are drawn to what are described as "shiny folks" as humans. These are typically the ones that are enjoyable to be around. However, these gleaming individuals are often not the ideal people to be around, since they appear to only be there if you can do something for them. Humans are also readily swayed by dramatic individuals. These are the folks that are always making noise and doing things they shouldn't be doing. It's thrilling and enjoyable. However, if they turn against you, it may be a painful experience. These individuals may be poisonous, and toxicity is the most effective way to destroy a bond. You want to hold on to these individuals because you believe they offer you joy, but the fact is that they are bringing you down. People usually feel bound to respond to the requests of attractive people—does this ring any bells? To identify a toxic buddy, simply attempt to do something for yourself or ask for a favour, and observe how they try to tear you down or refuse to cooperate.

This is when magic enters the picture. Magic will attract the correct kind of pals so that you may form long-lasting bonds with them and not have to worry about them leaving your life because you've reached a life milestone and can't take them to the mall twenty times a week any more. Instead, these people will cheer you on, urge you to be the greatest version of yourself, and will not blink an eye when you accomplish anything to better your life.

Magic will assist you in finding the love of your life as well as someone who will bring you soup when you are unwell.

You'll attract the sort of person who doesn't care if you're wearing your jammies all day or a $300 dress when they see you. These pals are hard to come by, but magic will bring them into your life.

This manner, you can be certain that you are establishing friends with the proper folks.

Assist You in Finding True Love - True love is the most difficult to discover. You may fall in love multiple times in your life, and you may even marry, but it is unlikely that it is eternal love. Love may be found everywhere and at any moment. True love, on the other hand, is difficult to locate since they are not seeking for the appropriate markers. They desire excitement and butterflies forever, and although those are great to share with your spouse twenty years from now, the butterflies will fade or not occur as regularly. When that happens, you want to be able to wake up and kiss the person next to you good morning while still feeling good about it.

How will you ever love them for the rest of your life if you don't? Find someone who, even after the butterflies go, keeps you joyful and gives you a pleasant sensation in your heart. True love is the kind of love that allows you to dispute all day and then laugh and be joyful for months on end. True love is waking up next to the person you love, seeing them at their most vulnerable, and loving them even more. This is the love that individuals strive for indefinitely, and it is a love that few people discover. Some are duped into believing they have discovered it because the butterflies linger longer than normal, then they marry, and five years later, they divorce.

This is due to the fact that they have just discovered someone they have lusted after for a longer period of time than usual. Then there's magic. Magic will send you someone who can make your heart race while still making you feel peaceful. It will bring you the one who will hold your hair while you're unwell and soothe your painful feet. It will bring you someone who will do your dishes for the rest of your life.

Someone who gets up with you at two a.m. to bake cookies because you can't sleep.

You want someone who supports the Wiccan religion and allows you to be yourself around them.

Once you let go and allow fate reveal you who you should genuinely be with, these spells will assist you strengthen your relationships while also forming a link with someone to develop an unbreakable partnership. The most difficult aspect is letting fate take over. You want to meet someone you like, but most individuals do not put their belief in fate since they already have someone in mind to be their eternal love. They do not want to give up that control for fear of losing anything. Will you fall in love with someone who is genuinely the one for you, or will you spend the rest of your life arguing with the person you married and casting endless spells to attempt to repair your relationship? The decision is all yours, but with a little patience and time, you will find the one you have genuinely been looking for.

Courage - If you are not exceptionally courageous in any element of your life, don't worry.

You are not alone yourself. The average individual has at least one area of their life where they lack guts. This might range from chatting to strangers to trying to climb the corporate ladder. Many aspects of life need bravery; it is difficult to be courageous enough for all of them on your own. For example, you could be able to go skydiving, but the notion of chatting to that stunning woman who has grabbed your attention absolutely frightens you.

That's okay since you can't be fearless in every situation. Maybe you're good at talking to people and public speaking, but you're frightened of riding in an elevator. There are various fears out there, and you cannot overcome them without bravery. Many people miss the power of magic and how it may improve your bravery levels. Courage is essential, and spells can help you get a little stronger. It is one of the most crucial qualities you may have as a witch since you will have to stand up to others. Many deeds need bravery, whether it is to preserve an ancient tree from a firm that wants to pull it down or to stop a dark witch from destroying someone's life.

Magic can assist, and it may provide you with much more than just a boost of bravery. Magic has the power to make you feel as if you can take on the world. You will feel as if you can accomplish anything, which is exactly what you desire. Just keep in mind that the results are not permanent, and you may need to reapply the spell a few times. After a few instances of learning how fantastic it feels to stand up to something that terrifies you, you will no longer need the spell since you will be able to be courageous on your own.

Luck - Luck is difficult to come by, yet many people require it. You need luck when you play the lottery, and you also need luck when you ask the love of your life to marry you, which is something that not many people consider. Luck, like bravery, is something you need to get by in life. It is not always necessary to rely on hard effort since hard work can only take you so far. In a large legal company, for example, you and the partner's pet are competing for a promotion. You may perform the more difficult tasks and put forth the most effort, yet they have an edge over you since they are a favorite. In this scenario, a little luck could come in handy. Instead of having a clear winner chosen out before the race even begins, luck might ensure that people are paying attention to your hard work.

You can build talismans and good luck charms with a few basic spells, or just surround oneself in a good luck aura with some spells; these spells are typically not difficult. The more luck you wish, however, the greater the witch you must be, for the stronger the witch, the more potent the spell. When you are stronger, you also have to "reapply" less frequently. What's more, there's a motive to practice, right? Everyone wants to be lucky, so work hard to become the greatest witch you can be.

A job interview is an example of a real-life scenario. You should cast these charms liberally since the more luck you have, the better off you will be at an interview, and you will hopefully obtain the job with ease. Don't be too arrogant; even if you apply and interview, if you're not a good fit, you might not get the job no matter how much magic you deploy.

Remember that there is a big difference between confidence and arrogance. Knowing you can perform the task gives you confidence. Being arrogant is believing that you can do something better than everyone else without any instruction. Cocky believes you are a lock for a job in which you have no prior experience. Confidence comes from understanding that you are a strong and quick learner who will be good at your work even without any instruction. You want to be self-assured while remaining humble. Recognize that you are not the ideal candidate for the job, but that you are the best prospect.

Mind Clarity - Have you ever had a burning question in your head or had to make a difficult decision? Did it take you longer than you'd want to acknowledge to accomplishing your goals with these scenarios? That occurs to everyone at some time in their lives, and it is very natural. You want to have a clean mind, which is more difficult to acquire than you would imagine.

Even if you clear your mind, it is often difficult to find a clear solution. You seek and search, yet everything has advantages and disadvantages.

This makes it difficult to find the time to accomplish what you want to do when you want to do it because you are still agonizing over the decision or trying to figure out everything—decisions may be messy.

If you're having difficulties deciding where you want to go in life, you can employ a spell to assist you figure it out. There are various spells that may help you expand your mind to make the proper decision, and a lot of them are related to Divination. Yes, prophecy may help you make better decisions since it gives you a sense of what the consequence of your choice will be. There are charms to help you cleanse your thoughts and spells to help you acquire the answers you need.

These are the spells you want to utilise to help you find your path in life and make the best decisions. Maybe you're wondering whether your husband is cheating on you and aren't sure if you should look into it. Cast a spell to acquire the answers you want. If they aren't cheating, don't feel bad about it. You are not considering their personal consequences, but rather conducting study before addressing them, like a sensible person would.

Getting Rid of Evil - Let's face it: we are frequently surrounded by evil. Without a question, this planet is a wicked playground. It is becoming more difficult to find a pure atmosphere in these times, and those who are decent are frequently attacked by the world. Have you ever felt that the entire 155 world was conspiring against you, and despite the fact that the bad individuals appear to be leading happy lives, you are unhappy? That is what many individuals face while attempting to live decent lives, because it appears that life does not desire good in it and rewards bad. There are techniques to keep oneself pure while also keeping your environment clean. Make sure you have a decent spot to work your magic. You want your thoughts to be free of attacks from other, bad witches as well.

There are various spells available for cleaning not just the surroundings but also your psyche.

Smudging is one of the most popular sorts of purifying spells.

Wicca: Herbal Magic discusses smudging. It is the process of burning a stick of herbs to cleanse an area or to achieve the effects of any number of spells. Herbs that are burned have a strong effect and build a magical barrier around you. This barrier is fantastic for the region where you choose to work your magic, but be sure to cleanse it on a regular basis because the barrier does not endure forever—unfortunately.

If you practice frequently, you should certainly smear your area before each spell, but if you just practice once a week or biweekly, once a week or biweekly should sufficient. Just be sure to cleanse it before casting a spell. The purer you maintain it, the more powerful your spells will be, and bad forces will be unable to oppose your spells. There are various different spells that you might employ to protect your mind and environment from the evil that lurks about. Candles are required for this (white candles especially). They provide you with pure energy to cast spells with. White candles act as a direct path to the Goddess herself, assisting you in keeping other beings from answering your calls. Although white candles are not required for most spells, it is advisable to light one every time you perform one.

Healing - As a Wicca novice, you can alleviate adverse effects and a variety of other ailments that exist underneath and on top of the skin's surface. You have the ability to assist those suffering from mental diseases. While some conditions cannot be cured, you can assist lessen symptoms such as sadness and anxiety. You can also assist someone suffering from PTSD in sleeping better at night. Magic is fantastic when utilised to aid others, including yourself. In addition, unlike pain and suffering from a significant physical injury, it does not require a lot of magical might to assist ease the symptoms of illnesses.

Prosperity - Have you ever been jobless and had to look for any kind of money simply to keep the lights on? It's not enjoyable, and it's becoming increasingly difficult to find work that pay the bills and put food on the table. That is the disadvantage of the world in which we live. Jobs are increasingly becoming digitized and outsourced. And, unless you live in a commune, you will need money to survive.

There are several spells available to assist you get an advantage in terms of prosperity. It is a good idea to collect a multitude of them so that you may shower yourself with luck and fortune if you ever need it. The same is true with healing spells.

Magic is a wonderful way to improve one's life. It will give you the boost you need to achieve great things in various areas of your life. Use Wicca magic to help you on your way here. You don't want to utilise it to make your life better. Put forth the work, and the magic will offer you an advantage you would not have had otherwise. That 156 is the loveliest aspect of Wicca magic. It is not intended to be a crutch, but rather a tool to assist you in succeeding.